FRANK COLEMAN

MY IRELAND

JOURNAL

MAD MOUNTAIN
PUBLISHING

ISBN 978-0-578-34455-3

Credits:
All photographs are originals by Frank Coleman.
Cover Photo: Rush, County Dublin, Ireland by Frank Coleman.
Title page clover © molodec www.fotosearch.ie

Cover and Interior Design by Cadhla Logan, Dublin, Ireland.

MAD MOUNTAIN
PUBLISHING

Ireland was a place for the renewal of hope and I still see it like that.
Daniel Day-Lewis

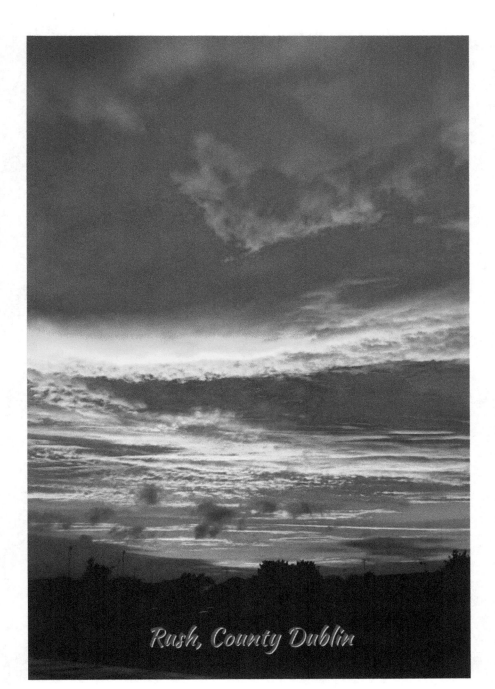

Rush, County Dublin

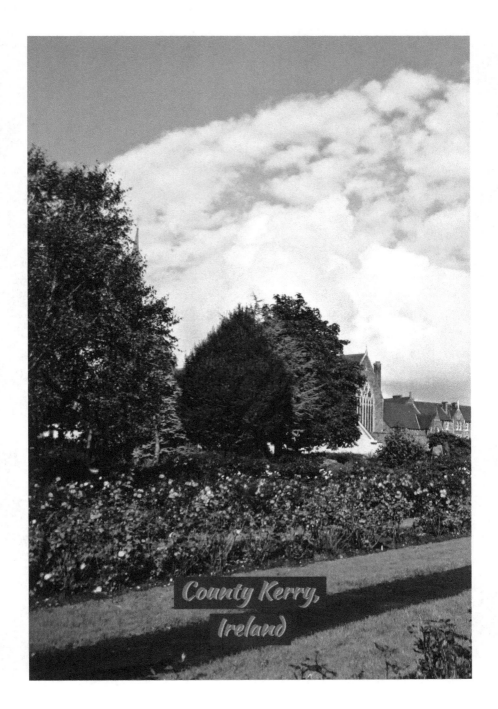

County Kerry,
Ireland

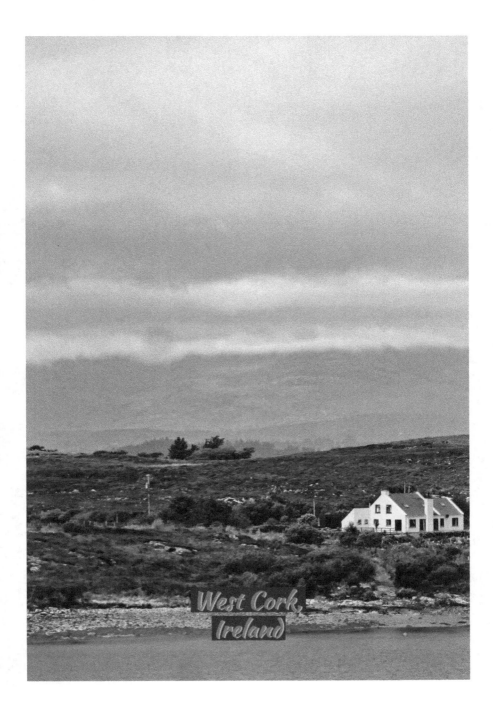

West Cork,
Ireland

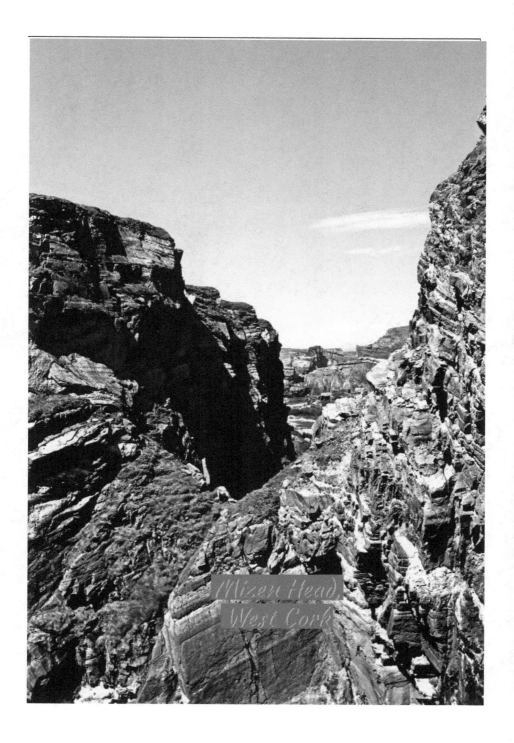

Mizen Head
West Cork

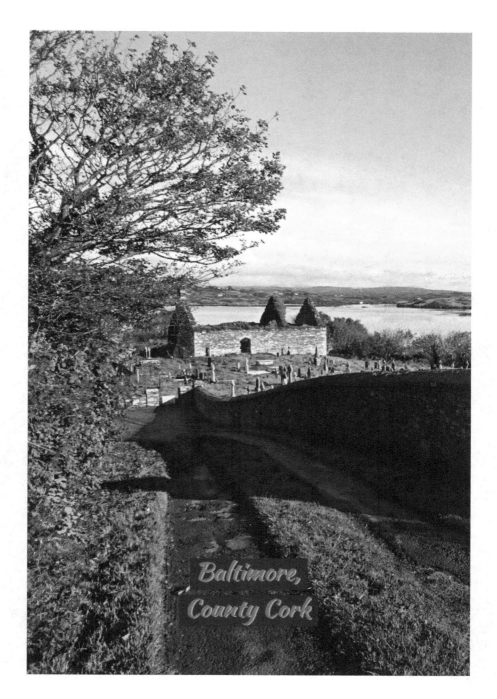

Baltimore,
County Cork

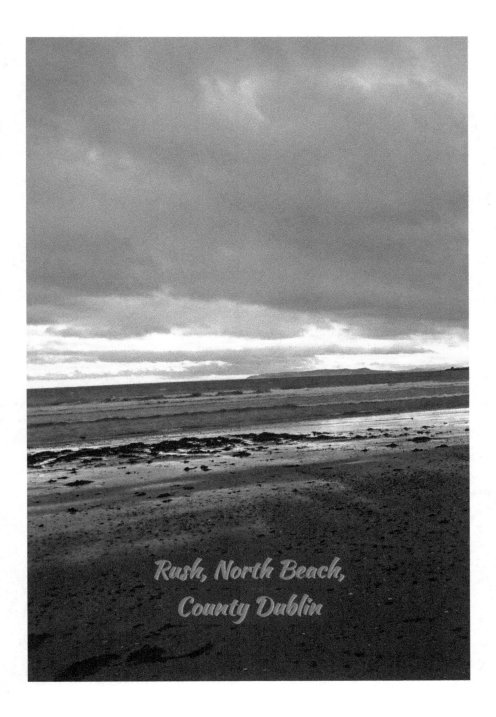

Rush, North Beach,
County Dublin

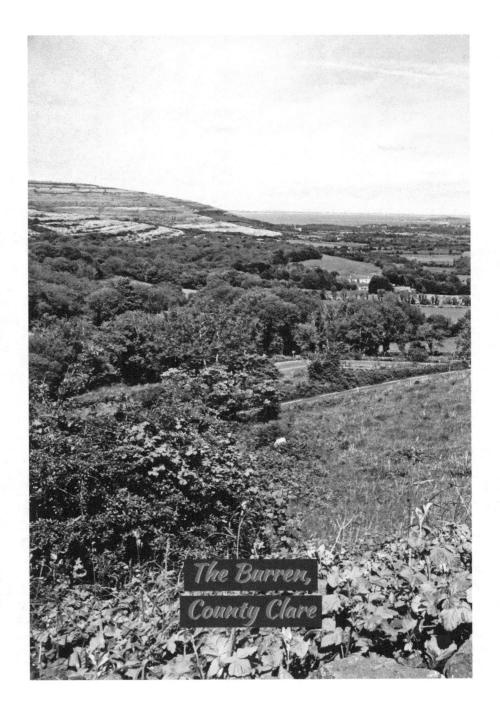
The Burren,
County Clare

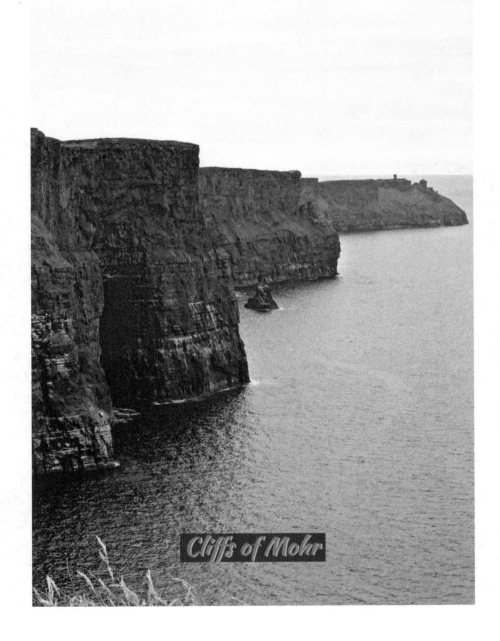
Cliffs of Mohr

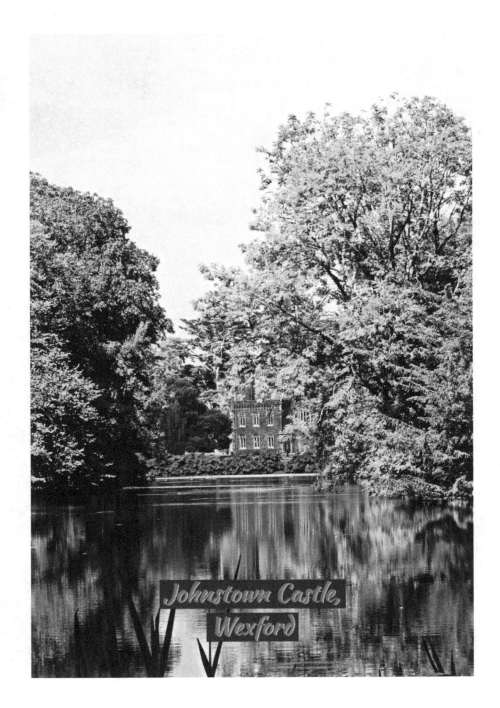

Johnstown Castle, Wexford

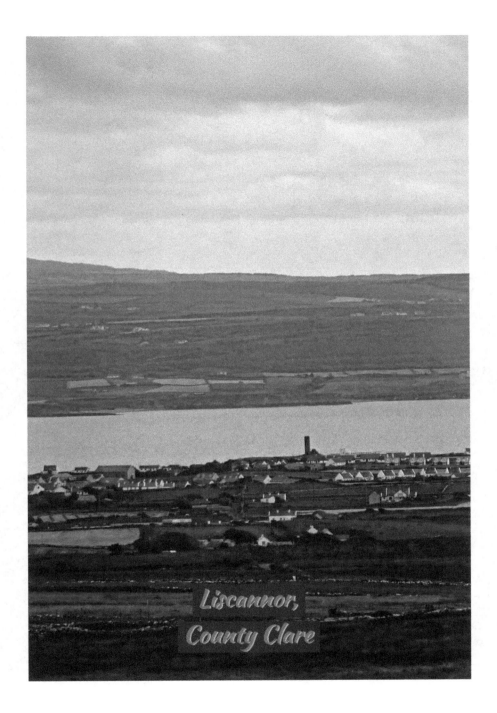

Liscannor,
County Clare

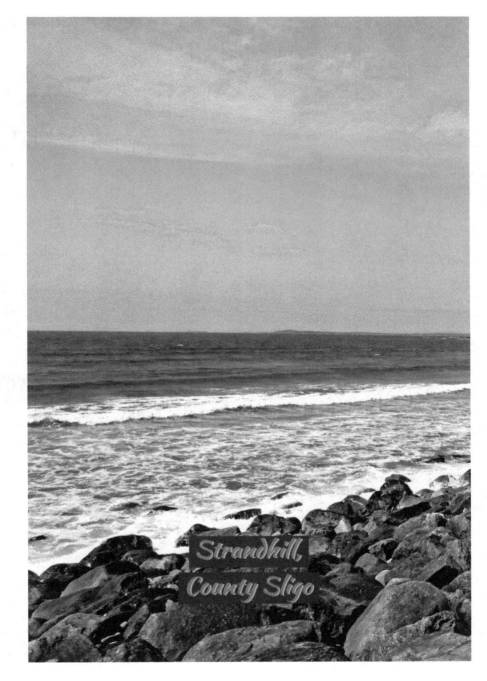

Strandhill,
County Sligo

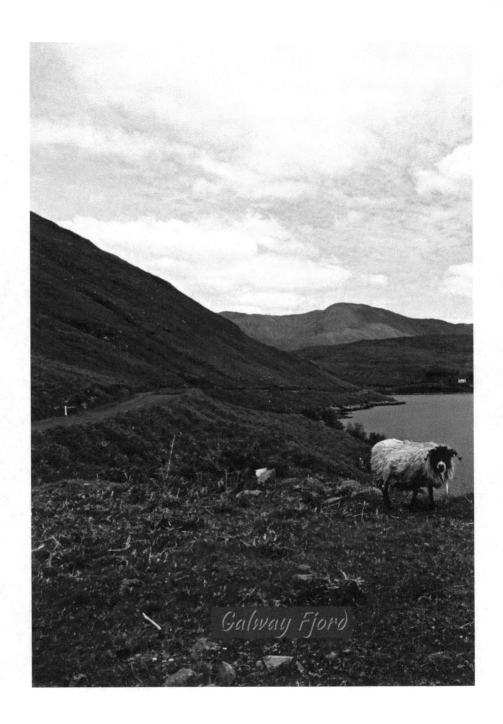

Galway Fjord

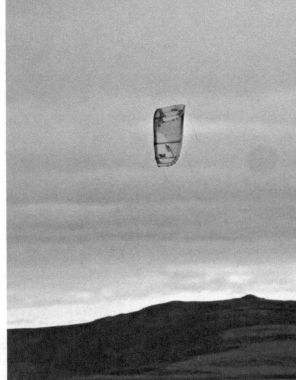
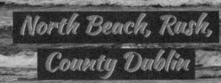

North Beach, Rush, County Dublin

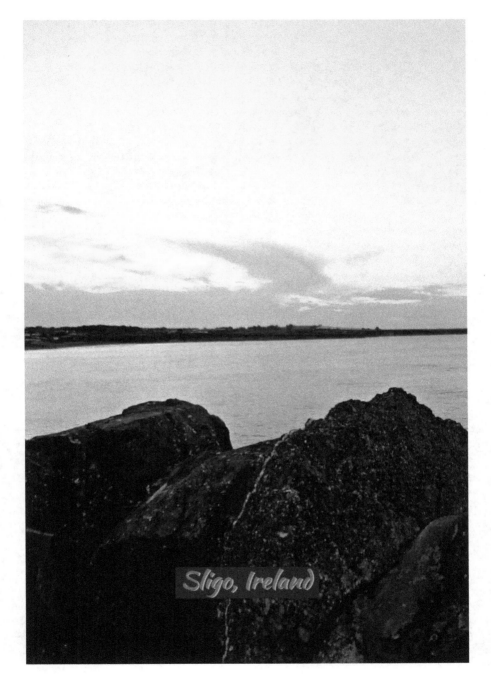
Sligo, Ireland

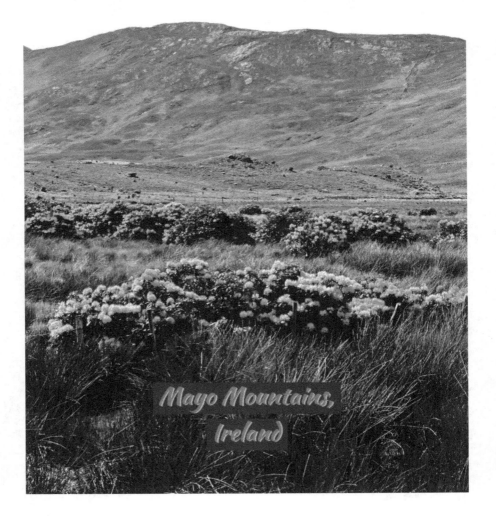

Mayo Mountains,
Ireland